Béisbol! Latino Heroes of Major League Baseball

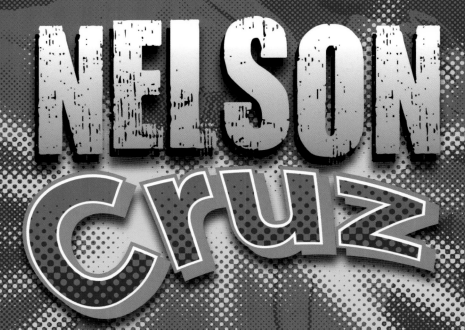

NELSON CRUZ

JOSH LEVENTHAL

WORLD BOOK

This World Book edition of *Nelson Cruz*
is published by agreement between
Black Rabbit Books and World Book, Inc.
© 2017 Black Rabbit Books,
2140 Howard Dr. West,
North Mankato, MN 56003 U.S.A.
World Book, Inc.,
180 North LaSalle St., Suite 900,
Chicago, IL 60601 U.S.A.

Design and Production by Michael Sellner
Photo Research by Rhonda Milbrett

Library of Congress Control Number: 2015954854

HC ISBN: 978-0-7166-9613-1   PB ISBN: 978-0-7166-9614-8

Printed in the United States at CG Book Printers,
North Mankato, Minnesota, 56003. PO #1797 4/16

Contents

CHAPTER 1

A Latino Legend

Nelson Cruz comes to bat. The bases are loaded. The score is 3 to 3 in the 11th inning. The pitch speeds toward the plate. Cruz is ready. He smashes it over the left-field wall. It's a **grand slam**!

Home Run Hitter

Cruz is an all-star baseball player. He is known for his great batting skills. He's also known for hitting home runs.

But Cruz wasn't always a pro ball player. He grew up in the Dominican Republic. He played basketball and baseball. And he helped in his uncle's car shop too.

Haiti

Dominican Republic

Number of Latino Major League Baseball Players

through 2015

642	Dominican Republic
341	Venezuela
253	Puerto Rico
193	Cuba
118	Mexico
55	Panama
17	Colombia
14	Curacao
14	Nicaragua
12	U.S. Virgin Islands
6	Bahamas
5	Aruba
4	Jamaica
3	Brazil
1	Belize
1	Honduras

CHAPTER 2

A Young Baseball Star

Cruz was born July 1, 1980. Young Cruz was a talented athlete. He played baseball in high school. He also played basketball for the Junior National Team.

Cruz was the star of his high school baseball team. Scouts came to the Dominican Republic to see him play. One scout wanted him to play for the New York Mets. Cruz's parents wanted him to finish high school first.

The Minor Leagues

The Mets and Cruz signed a contract on February 23, 1998. In 2000, the Mets traded Cruz to another team. Until 2005, Cruz moved from team to team. He worked on improving his skills in the **minor leagues**.

Cruz finally got his shot at a pro game on September 17, 2005. He played outfield in eight games for the Brewers that season.

Cruz's first major league hit was on September 28, 2005.

It was a **double** against the Reds. He also scored a **run**.

Canada

United States

Washington

2

16

California

6

4

Arizona

11

1

Oklahoma

12

Texas

13

5

10

14

Cruz has played baseball for many different teams.

Mexico

isconsin

9

3

Maryland

15

Illinois

8

Tennessee

7

Alabama

1 2001 Arizona League Athletics
2 2002 Vancouver Canadians
3 2003 Kane County Cougars
4 2004 Modesto A's
5 2004 Midland RockHounds
6 2004 Sacramento River Cats
7 2005 Huntsville Stars
8 2005-2006 Nashville Sounds
9 2005 Milwaukee Brewers
10 2006-2013 Texas Rangers
11 2008 Arizona League Rangers
12 2007-2010 Oklahoma City Redhawks
13 2010-2011 Frisco RoughRiders
14 2011 Round Rock Express
15 2014 Baltimore Orioles
16 2015 Seattle Mariners
17 2006-2009, 2012 Gigantes del Cibao

Dominican Republic

17

CHAPTER 3

In the  Majors

Cruz was traded to the Rangers in July 2006. He knocked his first major league homer on July 31. Cruz played 41 games for the Rangers in 2006. He played 96 games in 2007, but he struggled when batting.

Cruz spent most of 2008 in the minor leagues. That year, he led his league with 37 homers and batted .341.

A batting average shows how often a player gets a hit. An average of .300 is excellent. Batting .400 is very rare.

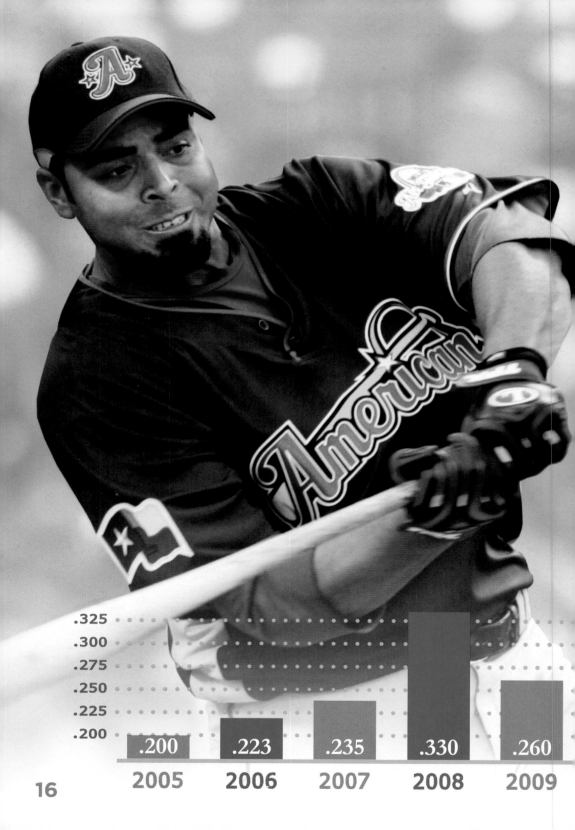

.325
.300
.275
.250
.225
.200

.200   .223   .235   .330   .260
2005   2006   2007   2008   2009

16

Becoming an All-Star

Cruz was named Texas' starting right fielder in 2009. In July, he was chosen for the All-Star Team. Cruz finished that year with a team-best 33 homers. He also had 20 stolen bases.

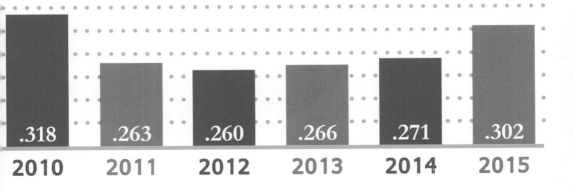

Cruz's Yearly MLB Batting Averages

.318	.263	.260	.266	.271	.302
2010	**2011**	**2012**	**2013**	**2014**	**2015**

World Series Bound

The Rangers made the **play-offs** in 2010. Cruz hit three home runs in the first round. His team went on to the World Series but lost.

Cruz and his team lost the World Series again the next year. But Cruz hit a record-tying eight homers in the 2011 **postseason**.

Eye on the Ball

right fielder

Fun Facts

6 feet
2 inches
(1.9 m) tall

right handed

WEIGHT

230
POUNDS
(104 kilograms)

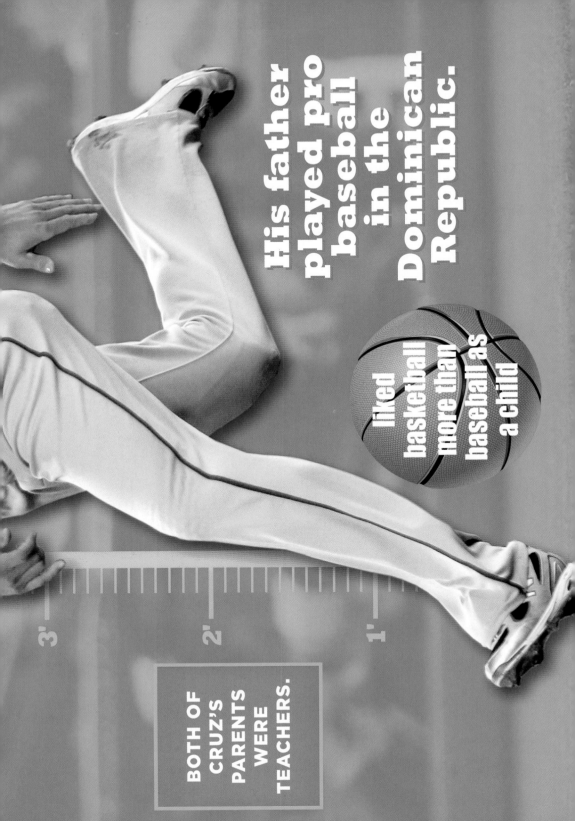

His father played pro baseball in the Dominican Republic.

liked basketball more than baseball as a child

BOTH OF CRUZ'S PARENTS WERE TEACHERS.

3'

2'

1'

CHAPTER 4

Continuing to

Cruz joined the Orioles in 2014. He led the league with 40 homers. He had a career-best 108 **runs batted in**.

After the season, he joined the Mariners. Cruz had his best season so far in 2015. He smashed 44 homers. He had 178 hits and a .302 average.

2014
Major League
Home Run
Leaders

Nelson
Cruz
40

Chris
Carter
37

Giancarlo
Stanton
37

Jose
Abreu
36

Mike
Trout
36

23

Runs ⌂ = 10 runs

Year	Runs
2005	1
2006	15
2007	35
2008	19
2009	75
2010	60
2011	64
2012	86
2013	49
2014	87
2015	90

Hits

Year	Hits
2005	1
2006	29
2007	72
2008	38
2009	120
2010	127
2011	125
2012	152

Games Played

2005	8	2008	31	2011	124	2014	159
2006	41	2009	128	2012	159	2015	152
2007	96	2010	108	2013	109		

Home Runs

0	6	9	7	33	22
2005	2006	2007	2008	2009	2010

29	24	27	40	44
2011	2012	2013	2014	2015

Runs Batted In

120
100
80
60
40
20
0

0	22	34	26	76	78	87	90	76	108	93
2005	2006	2007	2008	2009	2010	2011	2012	2013	2014	2015

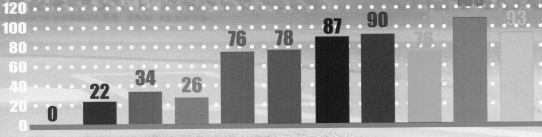

110	166	178
2013	2014	2015

Powerful Player

Cruz is a powerful baseball player. He has hit at least 20 homers every year since 2009. He has been an All-Star four times. Cruz is one of the best players in Major League Baseball.

Cruz's nickname is "Boomstick" for his powerful batting.

Timeline

1980

July

Cruz is born.

1998

February

signs with the Mets

2004

December

joins the Brewers

2005

September

plays first MLB game

28

2015

April

hits
200th
home
run

2014

February

joins the
Orioles

December

joins the
Mariners

2006

July

joins the
Rangers

August

hits first
grand slam

double (DUH-buhl)—a hit in baseball that allows the batter to reach second base

grand slam (GRAND SLAM)—a home run with players on every base

Latino (luh-TEE-no)—from Mexico or a country in South America, Central America, or the Caribbean

minor league (MY-nur LEEG)—a professional baseball organization that competes at levels below the major leagues

play-off (PLAY-ahf)—a series of games played after the regular season to decide which player or team is the champion

postseason (POST-see-suhn)—games played after the regular season

run (RUN)—when a player safely crosses home plate before the team has three outs

runs batted in (RUNZ BAT-ud IN)—when a player's at-bat causes one or more players to score a run

BOOKS

Gilbert, Sara. *Baltimore Orioles.* World Series Champions. Mankato, MN: Creative Education, 2013.

Kelley, K. C. *Baseball Superstars 2015.* New York: Scholastic Paperback Nonfiction, 2015.

Monnig, Alex. *Texas Rangers.* Favorite Baseball Teams. Mankato, MN: Child's World, 2014.

WEBSITES

Baseball
www.ducksters.com/sports/baseball.php

Nelson Cruz
m.mlb.com/player/443558/nelson-cruz

Seattle Mariners
seattle.mariners.mlb.com

INDEX